Tools We Use
Librarians

Dana Meachen Rau

Marshall Cavendish
Benchmark
New York

Books are so much fun to read!

A librarian can help you find books.

Libraries are filled with shelves.

Shelves help a librarian keep the books in order.

The librarian uses a computer.

The computer tells her where to find a book.

Librarians can help you find movies.

They can help you find magazines.

They can help you look at maps and globes.

They can help you listen to music.

Story time!

The librarian acts out
a story.

She helps the children learn a craft.

They use scissors, glue, and lots of paper.

The librarian gives you a library card.

This card lets you *borrow* books.

She uses a *scanner* to read the book's bar code.

Now you can bring the book home.

You bring books back on your next visit.

The book drop holds the books you return.

If the Deposit Box is full,
please do not stuff books in
the slot.
Thank you.

LIBRARY
BOOK RETURN

A librarian puts the books back.

She loads the books onto her cart.

She reads the code on a book's *spine*.

It tells her where the book belongs.

Librarians use many tools
to do their jobs.

They make sure the library
is always ready for you.

Tools Librarians Use

book drop

cart

computer

library card

scanner

shelves

Challenge Words

borrow (BAR-oh) To take something for a short time and return it.

scanner (SKAN-uhr) A tool that can read a bar code on a book.

spine (SPINE) The part of a book that faces out when the book stands on a shelf.

Index

Page numbers in **boldface** are illustrations.

About the Author

Dana Meachen Rau is an author, editor, and illustrator. A graduate of Trinity College in Hartford, Connecticut, she has written more than one hundred fifty books for children, including nonfiction, biographies, early readers, and historical fiction. She lives with her family in Burlington, Connecticut.

With thanks to the Reading Consultants:

Nanci Vargus, Ed.D., is an Assistant Professor of Elementary Education at the University of Indianapolis.

Beth Walker Gambro received her M.S. Ed. Reading from the University of St. Francis, Joliet, Illinois.

31

Marshall Cavendish Benchmark
99 White Plains Road
Tarrytown, New York 10591-9001
www.marshallcavendish.us

Library of Congress Cataloging-in-Publication Data

Rau, Dana Meachen, 1971–
Librarians / by Dana Meachen Rau.
p. cm. — (Bookworms. Tools we use)
Summary: "Introduces the tools librarians use in their work"—Provided by publisher.
Includes index.
ISBN 978-0-7614-2662-2
1. Librarians—Juvenile literature. 2. Libraries—Juvenile literature. I. Title. II. Series.
Z682.R327 2007
020.92—dc22
2006035147

Editor: Christina Gardeski
Publisher: Michelle Bisson
Designer: Virginia Pope
Art Director: Anahid Hamparian

Photo Research by Anne Burns Images

Cover Photo by *Jay Mallin Photos*

The photographs in this book are used with permission and through the courtesy of:
Jay Mallin Photos: pp. 1, 5, 7, 9, 11, 17, 19, 21, 23, 25, 28 (all pics), 29 (all pics).
Corbis: p. 3 Royalty Free; p. 15 Laura Dwight; p. 27 Patrick Pleul/dpa.
SuperStock: p. 13 age fotostock.

Printed in Malaysia
1 3 5 6 4 2